HOCKEY

How to Play the All-Star Way

By **Lisa Harris**

Introduction by **Cory Robinson**

Illustrated by **Art Seiden**

Photographs by **Frank McGady**

★ An **Arvid Knudsen** book ★

RSVP

RAINTREE STECK-VAUGHN

PUBLISHERS

The Steck-Vaughn Company

Austin, Texas

Acknowledgments

Photographs on pp. 11, 14, 29, 34, 39, and 40 from the
collection of Frank McGady. Photographs on pp. 4, 6, 8, and 22
from the collection of Sports Press Service.
Photographs on pp. 18, 32, and 36 from the
collection of Bruce Bennett Studios, Inc.
Editorial thanks to Norman Maclean, Jr. for
vital assistance in the securing of photographs.

Published by Raintree/Steck-Vaughn Publishers,
an imprint of Steck-Vaughn Company

Library of Congress Cataloging-in-Publication Data
Harris, Lisa.
Hockey/written by Lisa Harris.
p.   cm. — (How to play the all-star way)
"An Arvid Knudsen book."
ISBN 0-8114-5781-8
1. Hockey—Juvenile literature. [1. Hockey.]
I. Title. II. Series.
GV847.25.H37 1994
796.962—dc20   93-23282 CIP AC

Printed and bound in the United States

1 2 3 4 5 6 7 8 9 0   99 98 97 96 95 94 93

CONTENTS

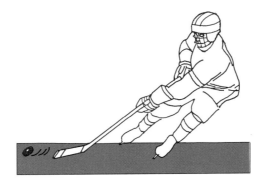

Wayne ▶ Gretsky, when signed to play for the Los Angeles Kings, brought increased interest and popularity to hockey in the United States.

◀ Wayne Gretsky at ten years old was already known as "The Great One" in his hometown, Brantford, Ontario. He has gone on to become one of the greatest players of all time.

INTRODUCTION

Hockey is two games. The first is skating. The second game consists of stickhandling, checking, and shooting. This is the superfast action you watch on television when the National Hockey League flashes across the screen.

Hockey is different from baseball, basketball, and football. Any good athlete can take a try at those sports. He or she doesn't need a lot of preparation for any of them. To play ice hockey you don't have to be tall or large. But you must first learn to skate. After you have mastered skating, the real fun starts.

Lisa Harris' book, "Hockey: How to Play the All-Star Way," is designed to show you what the sport is all about. It stresses the basics. It has real value for those who have been playing the game a while. It is perfect for beginners.

Hockey has a great deal to offer the young athlete. However, it will require teamwork, making decisions, and setting goals. It is a contact sport. Injuries and penalties are part of the game. But you can avoid them with enough care. Come on out on the ice! Fun and excitement await you.

— Cory Robinson
Head Coach
Hudson Catholic High School
Jersey City, N.J.

Baron Stanley, governor general of Canada, donated the Stanley Cup to the best amateur team in 1893. Montreal won the first competition for the cup.

A BIT OF HOCKEY HISTORY

Hockey began in Canada 100 years ago. Native Americans played games on frozen rivers. They passed a disk, called a puck, along the ice. The players used sticks. Almost all professional players used to come from Canada. Today, hockey stars also come from Sweden, Russia, Finland, Czechoslovakia, and the United States. Hockey is played all over the world. Teams play for gold medals at the Olympics and World Championships. The Canada Cup is an international tournament for professional players. The Stanley Cup is the championship trophy for the National Hockey League in North America.

American teams won the Olympic gold medal in 1960 and 1980. Each time, hockey became even more popular. American interest in hockey jumped again in 1988. That year Wayne Gretzky, the biggest name in hockey, joined the Los Angeles Kings. American television began showing more hockey games. Newspapers carried more hockey stories. Hockey is reaching everywhere in the United States, not just in the frozen north. Even tropical Florida has a professional hockey team.

In 1924, the Boston Bruins became the first National Hockey League team in the United States. They were one of the NHL teams still called the "Original Six." The others were the Montreal Canadiens, Toronto Maple Leafs, Detroit Red Wings, New York Rangers, and Chicago Blackhawks.

The Canadiens have been the most successful team in all of North American sports. They are considered a dynasty. A dynasty is a team that wins a championship for many years in a row. Montreal is the only team to build two dynasties.

Montreal was the only team in NHL history to win five straight Stanley Cups. They won the Stanley Cup each year from 1956 through 1960. And they won four every year from 1976 through 1979. There is a popular saying in hockey that every true hockey fan has two teams: his or her own and the Montreal Canadiens. The Canadiens have the most players and coaches honored in the Hockey Hall of Fame.

The Stanley Cup, more than 100 years old, is the most famous trophy in sports.

Montreal is the capital of professional hockey. In the United States Minnesota is the home of high school hockey. It has more hockey teams than any other state. In the United States, many young hockey players go to college to play hockey. The best players can go to college on a hockey scholarship if their grades are good.

Get to know about great players of the past, like Gordie Howe, who was Wayne Gretzky's idol, or Maurice "Rocket" Richard and Bobby Orr. You will learn a lot about the game. These players were as big in their day as Wayne Gretzky, Brett Hull, and Mario Lemieux are today.

Pro hockey today is a full-time job for the players. Training camp begins in September. The Stanley Cup final can last until June. Teams play 80 games during the regular season. The post-season play-offs last another two months. The Most Valuable Player in the regular season wins the Hart Trophy. The best post-season player is given the Conn Smythe Trophy.

College teams play shorter seasons and fewer games from October until March. There is a national college championship game between the final two teams. The best college players are named to the All-America team. The best player in United States college hockey is awarded the Hobey Baker Award.

High school seasons are different in each state. Many states hold play-offs for state championships.

HOW TO GET STARTED

USA Hockey is based in Colorado Springs, Colorado. This group directs amateur hockey in the United States. CAHA (Canadian Amateur Hockey Association) directs amateur hockey in Canada. USA Hockey runs programs and clinics throughout most of the country.

USA Hockey is the way to begin playing organized hockey in the United States. Call your local ice-skating rink to find out about registration. Rinks hold registration for USA Hockey membership cards. They give tryouts for league teams, too.

Some rinks of the country have "house" leagues. Many teams share the same rink. One area may have an all-star type of traveling team. That team plays another area's top team.

There are age ranges for all levels of amateur hockey. Some special players play at their talent level. If you are the next Wayne Gretzky or Mario Lemieux, you may end up playing with older kids. Your coaches and USA Hockey district directors can help you choose your level.

Rules may be different from one place to another. Girls' hockey may be run separately from boys' hockey. Age groups have the same names all over the country. But within an age group, the groups in

Moving the puck up the ice ▶

each level may vary. One district may have Squirts A, B, and C. Another district can have AAA, AA, and A.

The American age divisions are under review by USA Hockey. The current ones are:

Mites, for ages 9 and under;
Squirts, for ages 10 and 11;
PeeWees, for ages 12 and 13;
Bantams, for ages 14 and 15;
Midgets, for ages 16 and 17;
Juniors, for ages 18 and 19;
and Seniors, for ages 20 and up.

USA Hockey membership allows you to take part in USA Hockey programs, tournaments, and clinics. You will receive a one-year subscription to American Hockey Magazine. You also get insurance.

What if you do not have an ice-skating rink near you? What if your rink does not have a hockey program? USA Hockey can help you find clinics. USA Hockey can also help you find people in your area who are also looking for a hockey program.

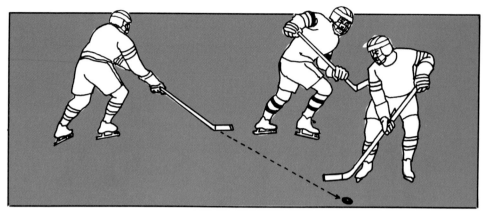

A backhand pass

For Membership

"If you don't know where to turn, call our member services and tell us where you're from," says a USA Hockey spokesman. "We'll get you started. If you don't have the experience, that's not a problem, we'll get you experience. If you can't even skate yet, we have learn-to-skate classes. If you're a kid in the middle of nowhere, we can take care of you."

To contact USA Hockey write to or call:

USA Hockey Member Services
4965 North 30th Street
Colorado Springs, Colorado 80919
(719) 599-5500

Your Physical Conditioning

Hockey is played in two-minute shifts. Players get to rest many times during the game. Even so, playing hockey is hard on your body.

Sleep: A young person needs more sleep than an adult. Taking a nap on game days may give you more energy.

Exercise: Skating is a good exercise for a hockey player. You can also build your muscles by jumping rope and swimming. If you need to work on your power, try running on skates. In the summer, you can run on sand or in water to build up your strength.

Nutrition: Hockey players burn off many calories. Cereals and potatoes give you more energy than candy and soda. Do not wait to eat at the rink before a game. The food at rinks is usually unhealthy for a player.

Equipment

Hockey can cost a lot of money. You need a lot of equipment. You can save money by buying used equipment. Check the bulletin boards at your rink to find good buys on used equipment.

Skates will be your biggest purchase. Skates must fit well and support your feet. All equipment for organized amateur hockey must be approved by the Hockey Equipment Certification Council (HECC).

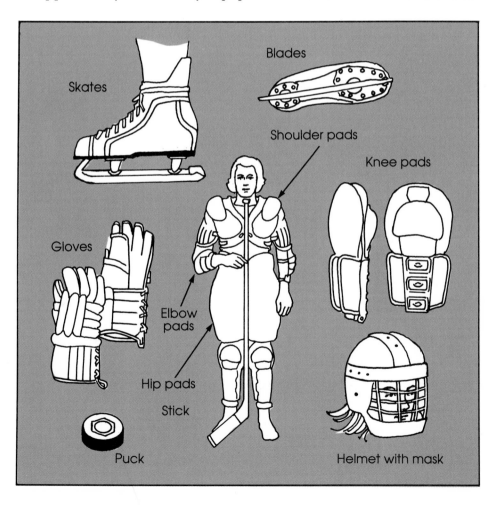

HOCKEY RINK

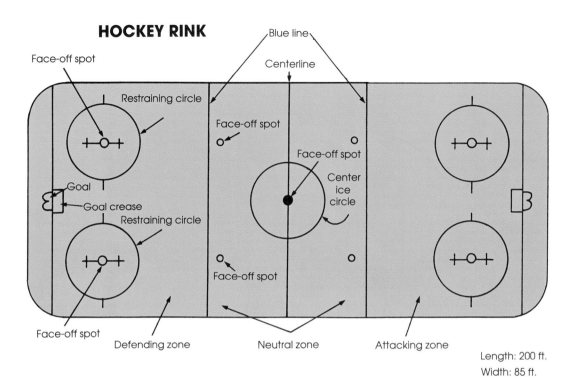

Face-off spot

Blue line

Centerline

Restraining circle

Face-off spot

Face-off spot

Center ice circle

Goal

Goal crease

Restraining circle

Face-off spot

Defending zone

Neutral zone

Attacking zone

Length: 200 ft.
Width: 85 ft.

HOW TO PLAY

Hockey is played on an ice rink. There is one puck in a game. It is passed with a stick from player to player. When your team has the puck, you are on offense. When the other team has it, you are on defense. Every player plays both offense and defense. The puck moves between teams very quickly. It is hard to control a rocklike piece of rubber flying around on ice at a hundred miles an hour!

Time

Hockey is played in three periods. In the pros each period lasts 20 minutes. The team with the most goals after three periods is the winner.

If the score is tied after the third period, there is overtime. The first team to score a goal wins the game. Overtime lasts for 5, 10, or 20 minutes. If no one scores in overtime, the game can end in a tie.

Face-Off

Each period of the game starts with a face-off in the center of the rink. Face-offs also take place after a goal has been scored. The game can be stopped for penalties or other reasons. When the game resumes, a face-off takes place near the spot where the puck was last in play.

Two opposing centers stand face-to-face. They hold their sticks and bend over at the face-off dot. Players must have one skate on each side of the line running through the face-off dot. This line is behind the line parallel to the goal line. During a face-off, the referee drops the puck. Then the centers go for it.

◀ Referee setting up a face-off

Once your team has the puck, you must move it forward. Move toward the goal. To go forward, you must stickhandle or pass. Passing forward is called "headmanning the puck."

Positions

At the start of a game, a team has six players on the ice: the center; two wingers or forwards—right winger and left winger; two defense-men—right defense and left defense; and goaltender (also known as netminder or goalie).

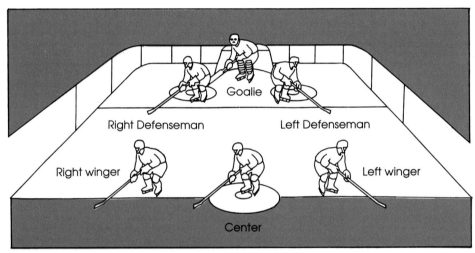

Each team has six players on the ice.

The Center

A center's job begins at the face-off. At the beginning of the game the two opposing centers meet at center ice and compete for the puck. They are engaged in a face-off. Face-off skills can often make the difference between quickly getting onto offense rather than defense.

A center's most important job is setting up plays. A center can score goals but is more valuable helping wingers score. A center must stay with the puck and direct the team's switch from offense to defense. That is why the center must be one of the best skaters on the team.

Wingers

Wingers support the center. They are linemates. Wingers play against the other team's wingers. Left wingers defend against the other team's right wingers.

All forwards must also help on defense. A left winger's main job is to score goals. You do not have to be left-handed to be a left winger. Great players have learned to shoot from their "off" wing. The off wing is the side opposite their natural shot.

The wing gets in position for a center's pass. This requires great speed. A winger must have energy. He or she needs speed to play the center's pass.

Defensemen

The nickname for defensemen is blueliners. This nickname tells you about a defenseman's most important job. The defenseman tries to keep the play from crossing his or her own blue line. If the opponents cannot cross into your zone, it will be hard to score. It will take at least a 60-foot shot for the puck to reach the net.

The offense's forwards have their job, too. They will cross the blue line when they can. That is when the defenseman's job becomes hard. With experience a blueliner will learn to block shots with his or her body. He or she clears the puck away from in front of the net. A blueliner also covers attackers. The defenseman also helps the goaltender. The defenseman blocks the shooter's view of the net. At the same time, the player must let the goaltender see what is going on.

Defensemen can pass the puck up to their forwards. Defensemen can follow the play into the offensive zone. They can also score.

Goaltender

A goaltender is sometimes called a netminder. His or her job is to prevent the puck from entering the net. If it does, the other team scores.

The goalie is the last line of defense. He or she has little to do with offense. A goalie who is a good stickhandler can pick up an assist. If the goalie passes to a teammate, it can lead to a goal. If the

In 1986, the Edmonton Oilers were eliminated from the Stanley Cup play-offs much earlier than expected. This happened because defenseman Steve Smith made a mistake. Smith shot the puck into his own net off goalie Grant Fuhr's leg. Smith went on to become an All-Star. But the "own-goal" ruined his twenty-first birthday. This misplay became part of hockey play-off history.

goalie is one of the last two players to touch the puck, he or she will get an assist. An assist by a goalie is rare. A goal by a goalie is even more rare.

Late in a losing game, the coach may need a sixth skater to help score a tying goal. Then the goalie comes off the ice. If the other team gets the puck, there will be no goalie protecting the net.

If a goal is scored when the goalie is away from the net, the goal is called an "open net" score. This goal will not count against the goalie's goals against average (gaa).

Scoring

A goal is scored when the puck crosses the goal line into the net. The goal scorer cannot kick or throw the puck into the net. If a shot rebounds off the body of a goaltender, it counts as a goal. If the puck bounces off a defender into the net, it counts as a goal. Each goal counts one point. The player who shot the puck in the goal gets one point.

A game that is tied at the end of regulation play goes into overtime play. Overtime usually is called "sudden death." That is because the first team to score wins the game.

What if your shot bounces off your teammate into the net? Then you get an assist on the play. The teammate who was in the way gets the goal. An assist is worth one point. An assist counts as much as a goal in your personal statistic. Setting up the goal is just as important as scoring the goal. A goal can be unassisted. A goal can also have two assists. The last two players whose sticks touch the puck both receive a point on their records for assisting the scorer.

The Coach

The coach is the boss of the team. He or she gets the team together. Your coach decides on who plays what position. He or she teaches young players the game.

The coach plans the plays and makes assignments. At game time, he or she is the strategist. The coach gives you pep talks and pats on the back when things go right and tells you why things go wrong.

Officials

Officials make sure the rules are followed in a hockey game. The chief official is the referee. He or she is in charge of starting the game. The referee wears a striped shirt. The referee's call is final. He or she can call penalties for breaking rules.

There are also linesmen. They work with the referee. They make some calls the referee is unable to make.

Skating

To play hockey, you have to skate. Good skating skills can make the difference between not making the team and becoming an All-Star. Make sure your skates fit properly. Your blades should be sharp. They should grip the ice. Dull blades will slide out of your control.

The blade of the skate has inside and outside edges. It feels like a flat surface with two distinct edges. It is not a single thin line teetering on the ice.

A good skater uses the skates' edges to turn, push off, and stop. From a standing start, use short strides. This will give you quick bursts of power. Once you start, you can take longer strides to save energy.

Some people have strong hips and legs. They do not have to dig in. They do not have to push off to get strength. If you are not a "smooth" skater, you must practice. Power skating can increase your speed and strength.

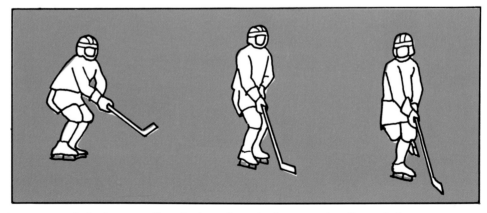

A skater uses the skate edges to turn, push off, and stop.

Power Skating

Power skating involves a constant push-off. You do not get much glide between strides. You have to bend your legs more to get better balance.

Power skating is hard work. But it is worth the effort. Luc Robitaille, an All-Star for the Los Angeles Kings almost did not make the NHL because he was a weak skater. He was chosen only after 170 other players. Robitaille's weak skating would have kept him from making the team. After Robitaille took power-skating lessons, he made the NHL All-Rookie team in his first season. He has averaged almost 50 goals a year. He has made the All-Star team many times.

Power skating needs a constant push-off.

Skating Tips

When you skate forward, think about each foot making half of a wide letter *V.* In going backward, the left foot makes a letter *C* with each stride. The right foot makes a backward *C.*

A hockey player has to skate in any direction. He or she must skate backward, forward, to the left, and to the right. A hockey player must move clockwise and counterclockwise.

Do not let being right-handed keep you from learning to move, turn, or stop to the left. Make sure you practice. Practice on the left and on the right sides. Practice all these skills on your weaker side. Practice until you no longer have a weaker side. Skating is only the first skill you need. When you can move around, get a hockey stick.

BASIC STICK SKILLS

The hockey stick has a shaft and a blade. The shaft is the long part where you place your hands. Players tape the shaft of their stick for a better grip. The blade is the short part at the bottom. It is the part that hits the puck. Players also tape the blade to control the puck.

Your top hand guides your stick. Wrap the thumb of your top hand around to the back of the shaft. This gives you control. Your shooting hand moves up and down the shaft. It is used for power. Your top hand must be still to direct your shots.

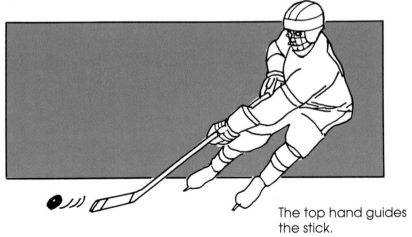

The top hand guides the stick.

Stickhandling

Guide the puck with the blade of your stick. This is called puck-carrying or stickhandling. Cradle the puck by tilting your blade over

◄ Mario Lemieux, the Pittsburgh Penguins superstar and NHL All-Star, is considered one of the most exciting players in the game today.

it. As you skate, move the puck gently from side to side. Keep it from moving out of your reach.

You have to watch where you are going. You also have to be aware of where your opponents and teammates are.

Keep your head up when you stickhandle. Handle the stick without help from the eye. Practice stickhandling by feel.

Train yourself not to look down. Make yourself an obstacle course. Weave between chairs or cones as you stickhandle. If you look down, you will knock into the chair or cone!

Passing

When you are passing, relax your hands. Then you can adjust to the impact when the puck hits the stick. The puck should meet the stick gently. If it meets the stick too hard, then it will bounce away. This will not happen if your grip is relaxed. It is like catching a baseball with a cupped hand.

Passing is done with the forehand or the backhand. There are many kinds of passes. There are straight passes, moving passes, or combination passes. Standing players often feed the puck to teammates moving 25 miles per hour.

What kind of pass should you make? Decisions are often made quickly. You can pass the puck hard. You can put the puck on a

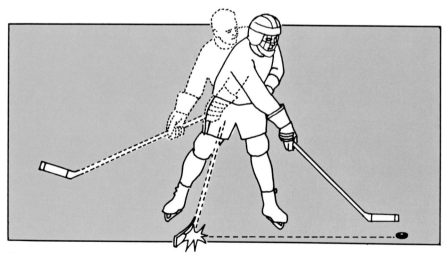

The power shot is made with a smooth, sweeping motion of the stick.

teammate's stick. You can "lead" a pass by sending it ahead of the moving receiver. It is like what a football quarterback does with a pass receiver. Always keep your head up. See what is going on. You may want to adjust your wrists to change the speed of your pass. You may want to switch directions.

The flip pass: Normally, you keep the puck on the ice to pass it. A flip pass lifts the puck up over the stick of a rival player between you and your receiver. A flip pass can be made forehanded or backhanded. It is often made off the toe of the blade.

Practice making the puck land flat. You can flip the puck by scooping it. Cup the puck by putting your stick blade over the puck. Flip it quickly with a flick of your wrists. You can also flip the puck by shoveling it. To do this, turn your stick out flat. Jab at it hard enough to lift it.

A drop pass

The drop pass: To make a drop pass, leave the puck for a teammate. Skate away. Try to be sure your teammate will get the puck before an opponent does. Do not push it. Your teammate may over-skate the puck.

Shooting

Shots can be taken from either side of the blade. All basic shots are either forehand or backhand. For a forehand shot, use the inside, curved part of the blade.

The backhand shot is taken with the back of the blade. The backhand is hard for a goalie to stop. Curved blades have kept shooters from using the backhand. Goalies hardly ever see a backhand. Wayne Gretzky and Mario Lemieux are backhand experts.

The slap shot: The slap shot is very exciting. Famous players, such as Bobby Hull of the Chicago Blackhawks, used to rip a slap shot 100 miles per hour. Al MacInnis of the Calgary Flames is famous for slap shots. They were so hard that the goalies could not react. Goalies could not do anything even when they knew what was coming.

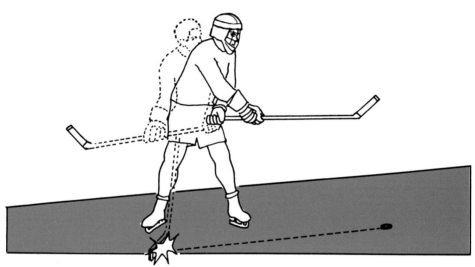

A slap shot

The slap shot is a shot on goal using a full arm motion. Wind up to draw the stick far back from the puck. Swing hard. The windup is like a golf swing.

A slap shot is useful as a weapon. It can freeze the goalie. A shorter backswing makes your shot less dramatic. But it gives the goalie less time to get ready. Watch NHL star Paul Coffey take a slap shot. He does not have to take a huge swing to unload a long shot. He scores goals by surprising the goalie.

At first, do not try for power when you practice slap shots. Work on accuracy. MacInnis and Coffey did not have that zing when they were Bantams. As they grew stronger, their shots became more powerful. Shoot for distance. When you are older and stronger, add the power.

Accuracy is a big problem with the slap shot. A slap shot must travel far at a high speed. It is harder to direct than a wrist shot. This is especially true when the puck is "one-timed," or made on the fly.

The one-time shot: On a one-time shot, you wind up as the puck is being passed to you. Your stick hits the puck while the puck is coming at you at full speed. Rhythm and timing are important for accuracy. A one-time shot is not meant to be a wild stab.

It takes two players to make a one-time shot successful. Practice with a friend. The puck has to be moving for you to one-time it. A linemate can feed you passes while you are moving. Then you can hit the puck past him or her.

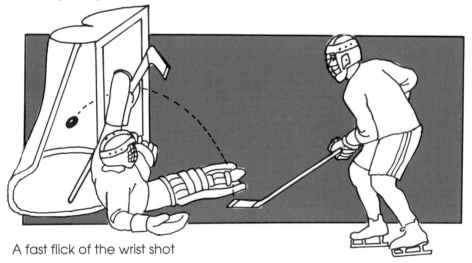

A fast flick of the wrist shot

The wrist shot: The wrist shot is a shot on goal taken without drawing the stick slightly behind the puck. A fast flick of the wrists lifts the puck. The wrist shot is fired without hesitation. It is taken from in close. The goalie has no warning. When the puck is against the blade, snap your wrists. Release this shot quickly to give it power.

The snap shot: The snap shot is a cross between a slap shot and a wrist shot. It is a shot on goal taken by moving the stick back slightly from the puck. Use a motion like the wrist shot. It is a mini slap shot from about 20 feet from the goal.

Use a short snap of your wrists. Bring your stick back an inch behind the puck. This adds a very short swing of the stick. Then move your wrists less than you would for a slap shot.

Practice directing the shot. The goalie can stop your shot if you direct it wrong. Practice aiming at a small spot in the net. Then aim at the goalpost without a goalie to practice shooting at a target. Skate and aim for the goalpost. Try to hit it five out of ten times.

Accuracy can depend on good balance. Make sure you have good balance. If you are a left-handed shooter, shoot while moving off your right foot. If you are a right-handed shooter, shoot when your weight is off the left foot.

With hands and feet in proper position, your stick can help you control the puck. Twist your stick blade faceup as the puck leaves the stick. Lift the stick so your shot rises. If you leave the edge of your blade even along the ice, the puck will not rise. To keep the puck along the ice, keep your wrists low on your release. Do not snap the puck up while shooting.

Brett Hull is the son of Bobby Hull, the legendary slap shot shooter. But Brett is famous for his snap shot. He has used it to lead the NHL in goals many times.

Shooting accuracy requires good balance.

CHAPTER

5

CHECKING

Hockey is very much a contact sport. It is often a collision sport. Hitting your opponent with your body is an important defensive skill. You can only bump the player who is carrying the puck. Checking means interrupting your opponent's movements. You can check with your body or with your stick.

Bodychecking

A body check is not like a football tackle. You do not throw your opponent down on the ice. You knock him or her away from the puck. You can bodycheck if you have good balance. You can shake off a body check with good balance. It is easier to bodycheck along the boards than at open ice. You can check him or her with your shoulder or your hip. You cannot take more than two strides to hit. More strides will get you a penalty. Bodycheck to get your opponent away from the puck.

Stick Checking

You can also check with your stick. Reach out with the blade of your stick. Push the puck off an opponent's stick. This is called a poke check.

A hook check is a longer, slower check. It is a good defensive play. Lay the shaft of the stick along the ice. Bend one knee. Put the other knee on the ice. Sweep your stick forward toward the puck to stop it.

An illegal check will receive a penalty.

A poke check

Strategy

Fore-checking: The team coverage in the opponents' zone is called fore-checking. It is an aggressive strategy designed to get possession of the puck. Fore-checking is used when your team is trailing and needs to score. Your coach knows when the team should fore-check.

Back-checking: The way your team covers your opponents in your zone is called back-checking. Back-checking is a defensive strategy that requires the whole team. You need to be alert, as you may switch from defense to offense in an instant.

A hook check

OFFENSE

The team that has the puck is on offense. It's job is to score. Offensive play involves more than just passing and shooting. Face-offs, stickhandling, and positioning are all jobs for the offense.

Offense in the defending zone

When your team gets possession of the puck in your own zone, your object is to move it into the neutral zone. This is breaking out. Your coach will teach you formations for breaking out quickly and effectively.

Offense in the neutral zone

In the neutral zone your team makes the shift from offense to defense. This is called transitional play. You will be doing a lot of stickhandling, passing, and skating to get the puck into shooting range. While you are on the attack at full speed, the defenders are trying to stop you. If you cannot successfully pass to a teammate, the only choice may be to dump the puck. This means unloading the puck and hoping a teammate gets to it.

If you have the puck and your teammate is in the slot — make a pass. Players who do not pass to teammates who are in better shooting positions can be benched for being selfish.

◄ Bobby Orr, who played mostly with the Boston Bruins, is considered the best defenseman of all time. With his great passing and skating skills he changed the way modern hockey is played.

A breakaway is an exciting part of the game.

Offense in the attacking zone

Offensive patterns have to be practiced. The action can get furious. The attackers swarm the net to try to score a goal.

While setting up to score, use the boards in the corners. You can make and get passes that rebound off the boards. Most goals are scored from the area between the face-off circles called the slot. When in the slot, try to be open for passes. You are in the best position to shoot for a goal.

Breakaways

Sometimes a team suddenly loses possession of the puck. Its defensemen are caught far from their goal. The offense then has a clear path. This is called a breakaway. A solo breakaway is when you are carrying the puck with no defender between you and the goaltender. A solo breakaway is considered the most exciting showdown in hockey. More common breakaways are made by two or three attackers exchanging passes with each other against one or two defenders.

Offensive play is fast, heavy-hitting action.

DEFENSE

When the opposing team is in your zone, every member of your team plays defense. But your team's defensemen have the most responsibility.

Defensemen play in pairs. One member of the pair is more responsible for starting the offense. He or she will take the puck out of the zone. This is the rushing defenseman. Most coaches match this player with a more cautious player. This defenseman is called a "stay-at-home" blueliner. He or she hangs back. If the team loses the puck, this defenseman can recover quickly.

One defenseman is like a quarterback in football. He or she can start a play off right. It is the defenseman who directs teammates into positions for passes. Defensemen who are not rushers want to get the puck to their forwards. Then their forwards can take the puck to the neutral zone, away from their goal. This stops the opponent's play before their goaltender is threatened.

When you practice your defensive moves, work with a friend. A defenseman must know his or her partner. A good defenseman can pick up a partner's pass easily. It is like catching something with your right hand that your left hand has dropped.

◀ Grant Fuhr, All-Star goalie for the Edmonton Oilers, is the first black Canadian in NHL history to play that position.

A defenseman must learn what to watch out for from an opponent. A defenseman can learn when an opposing forward is going to shoot. The attacking forward may look down just before shooting the puck. When the forward looks down, the defenseman can move closer to him or her. Then the puck will bounce off the defenseman's pads. But the forward should not move too quickly. The forward can hit a defenseman in the face with a shot if the forward sees the defenseman coming. The best place for a goal shot is the slot.

Offensive players must be forced to the sides. They should be kept away from the net.

Goaltending

Players become goaltenders for many reasons. Some goalies wanted to play hockey but could not skate well. Still other people love the pressure of goaltending.

A goalie can be small. Fast reflexes can make up for a smaller size goalie. A big goalie can block the net just by standing there. A small goalie moves from side to side.

A goalie needs a big glove with a deflector, called a blocker, over the forearm to stop the puck. Stopping the puck is called a save. Goalies have full masks. The mask protects their faces from flying pucks. Their pads cover their legs. A goalie's legs are always hitting the ice and stopping the pucks. A goalie's stick has a wider blade to stop the puck.

The goalie is the only player who can use his or her hands. A goalie can catch the puck without penalty.

A goaltender's typical defensive stance in front of the net

The puck-handler cradles the puck while looking up ice.

An attacker coming around the net

CHAPTER

8

SPECIAL TEAMS

The penalty box is at the side of the rink. The referee calls a penalty when a player has broken a rule. Then the player is put out of the game, and he or she must leave the ice. The player sits in the penalty box for two minutes for a minor penalty. The player loses at least five minutes for a major penalty.

Penalty Killers

The team whose player is in the penalty box is short-handed. The short-handed team calls in its best defensive players. These players are called "penalty killers." The players left on the ice must work extra hard. Sometimes the team can be short two players due to penalties.

Power Plays

When one team has more players on the ice due to a penalty, that team is on the power play. Offensive players will try to take advantage of this to score. Offensive players are called the "power play unit." The "penalty killers" and the "power play unit" are both called "special teams." The players on the special teams are used to playing together. The offensive players on a special team will want to make a goal. If the team scores, it is called a power-play goal. It is easier to score goals when the defense is short-handed.

No team's power play scores all the time. On a power play the special team quickly moves into the other team's zone. Even if they do not score, they may wear down some of the defensive players.

Common Penalties and Signals

The referee has the final decision for all parts of the game. If a rule is broken, the referee will call a penalty. Most penalties will cause a team to play shorthanded for two minutes or more. The following are some common calls:

Tripping: Pulling an opponent down with a stick, knee, foot, arm, or hand (2 min.)

Slashing: Hitting an opponent with the stick (2 or 5 min.)

Misconduct: Using bad language with an official (10 min., team not short on ice)

Slow whistle: Signal that the referee will call a penalty once the offending team controls the puck

Washout: When used by the referee, it means the goal was not allowed. When used by a linesman, it means there is no icing or offside.

Bench penalty: Given for bad language or other bad conduct on the bench (2 min.)

Boarding: Checking a puck carrier into the boards too roughly (2 or 5 min.)

Butt-ending: Pushing the butt end of the stick into an opponent (5 min.)

High-sticking: Carrying a stick above the shoulder into or close to an opponent (2 or 5 min.)

Match penalty: An offending player is put out of game. A teammate serves 5 or 10 min. on the penalty bench depending on the rule broken.

Penalty shot: Given to a player who is fouled from behind on a clear break-away, or when a defensive player other than the goalie falls on the puck in the crease. The puck is placed on the center face-off spot. An offensive player is allowed to take one shot at the goal. He or she may skate with the puck in any direction. But once over the blue line, the player must head directly to the goal. Only the goaltender defends against a penalty shot.

Roughing: Unnecessary roughness (one or two 2 min. penalties)

Spearing: Pushing the blade of the stick into an opponent (5 min.)

Too many men: Given for having too many men on the ice (2 min.)

Delay of game: Any deliberate attempt to delay the game (2 min.)

Fighting: Hitting with fists (one or two 2 min. penalties, or 5 min.)

SOME REFEREE SIGNALS

Elbowing: Driving an elbow into an opponent (2 or 5 min.)

Holding: Holding on to an opponent in any manner (2 min.)

Charging: Taking two or more strides before hitting an opponent (2 or 5 min.)

Cross-checking: Holding a stick with both hands and pushing the handle into an opponent (2 or 5 min.)

Interference: Blocking an opponent who does not have the puck (2 min.)

Icing: Signal used by a linesman for illegal shooting of a puck all the way across the ice

Hooking: Using a stick as a body "hook" to block an opponent (2 min.)

Delayed calling of penalty: When any team has three players serving penalties at the same time

43

The penalty shot gives a player a clear shot at the goal with only the goalie to defend.

Icing

Shooting the puck all the way across the ice is illegal most of the time in hockey. It is called icing. A player must move the puck with the stick. The player can also pass the puck to a teammate. When killing penalties, icing is legal. The defending team can send the puck across the ice.

Final Word

Reading about hockey can teach you a lot. Watching professionals playing the game can also teach you. But it is out on the ice that you learn the real game of hockey. This is the only way to know the thrill of stickhandling the puck, passing, or shooting a goal and checking an opponent. Most of all, hockey teaches you how to be part of a team. What you learn will stay with you always. Being an unselfish player will make you a star to your teammates. Being a true sport will win you respect.

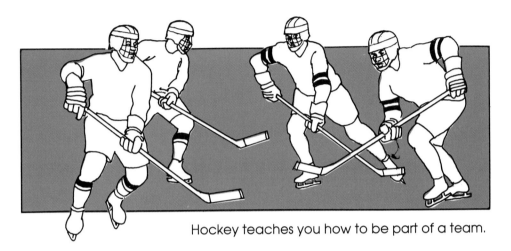

Hockey teaches you how to be part of a team.

GLOSSARY

Assist: A scoring credit to the one or two players who last passed the puck to the player who shot a goal, worth one point

Back-check: Covering an opponent in your own zone

Blue line: One-foot-wide blue line painted across the ice 60 feet from each goal. Blue lines divide the rink into attacking, neutral, and defending zones.

Blueliner: Nickname for a defenseman

Body check: Legal hit of an opponent with your body in order to take him or her out of the play

Breakaway: Attacking, ahead of all defenders, with a clear path to the goalie

Center: The middle position on a three-man forward line; also the act of moving the puck toward the middle for better positioning

Center ice: Neutral area between blue lines

Clearing the puck: The defending team getting the puck away from in front of its goal

Crease: 4-foot by 8-foot rectangle in front of the goal where attacking players cannot enter without possession of the puck

Cross-checking: Illegally striking an opponent with a stick held completely off the ice by two hands

Face-off: The drop of the puck by an official to start or

restart play; also called a draw

Face-off circle: Circular area painted on the ice for the purpose of holding a face-off

Flip pass: Pass made by lifting the puck over an opponent's stick to a teammate

Fore-checking: Covering your opponent in your offensive zone to prevent the other team from attacking

Forwards: Collective name for centers and wingers

Goal: Awarded when the puck crosses the line painted on the ice in front of the net; worth one point

Goal judge: Official who sits behind the net off the ice. He or she indicates whether a goal was scored by turning on a light.

Goaltender: Player who guards the net; also called netminder, goalkeeper, or goalie

Hook check: Legal sweep of the stick along the ice to intercept or prevent an opponent's pass

Icing: Shooting the puck from behind the red centerline across the opponent's goal when there is no intended receiver. This move is illegal.

Linesmen: Officials working with the referee, responsible for some calls, such as icing

Major penalty: Penalty for a violation of rules deemed major, such as fighting. The offending player must sit in the penalty box for five minutes.

Match penalty: Removal from the game for a violation of the rules, such as trying to injure an opponent

Minor penalty: Penalty for a violation of rules deemed to be minor, such as holding or tripping an opponent. The offending player must sit in the penalty box for two minutes.

Overtime: Extra session of a game played only if the score is tied after regulation play is over

Penalty box: Section at the side of the rink where offending players must stay during a penalty

Penalty killers: Players who are on the ice while their team is shorthanded because of a penalty

Penalty shot: A one-on-one shot on goal when the skater faces only the goalie and no defender. It is awarded in extreme situations when a player is tripped from behind in the act of shooting. The shooter can skate in on the goalie from the red line.

Point: An area on the ice inside the blue line where a power play is usually organized

Pointman: The leader of a power play; usually a defenseman beginning action from the point

Power play: A period of time when one team has a manpower advantage because the other team has been penalized; also a collective term for the players a team uses during a power-play situation.

Power-play goal: A goal scored during a power play

Regulation: The three periods of the game, usually totaling 60 minutes. USA Hockey leagues play shorter periods for very young kids.

Save: A stop by the goal-tender, made with a glove, stick, blocker, or skate

Short-handed: Being at a manpower disadvantage because of a penalty

Stickhandling: Guiding the puck with the stick

Unassisted goal: A goal scored when no teammates are credited for assisting. Worth one point on a player's record

Wrist shot: A shot on goal taken without drawing the stick slightly behind the puck but by flicking the wrists to lift the puck

FURTHER READING

Gutman, Bill. *Ice Hockey*. Marshall Cavendish, 1990

McGuire, William. *The Stanley Cup*. Creative Education, 1990

Solomon, Chuck. *Playing Hockey*. Crown Books, 1990

Ward, Carl. *Hockey*. Sterling, 1991

INDEX